GOALS AND GOAL SETTING

Larrie Rouillard

A FIFTY-MINUTE™ SERIES BOOK

CRISP PUBLICATIONS, INC.
Menlo Park, California

GOALS AND GOAL SETTING

Larrie Rouillard

CREDITS:
Editor: **Elaine Brett**
Layout and Composition: **ExecuStaff**
Cover Design: **Carol Harris**
Artwork: **Ralph Mapson**

Copyright © 1993 Crisp Publications, Inc.
Printed in the United States of America by Bawden Printing Company.

English language Crisp books are distributed worldwide. Our major international distributors include:

CANADA: Reid Publishing, Ltd., Box 69559—109 Thomas St., Oakville, Ontario Canada L6J 7R4. TEL: (416) 842-4428; FAX: (416) 842-9327

AUSTRALIA: Career Builders, P.O. Box 1051, Springwood, Brisbane, Queensland, Australia 4127. TEL: 841-1061, FAX: 841-1580

NEW ZEALAND: Career Builders, P.O. Box 571, Manurewa, Auckland, New Zealand. TEL: 266-5276, FAX: 266-4152

JAPAN: Phoenix Associates Co., Mizuho Bldg. 2-12-2, Kami Osaki, Shinagawa-Ku, Tokyo 141, Japan. TEL: 3-443-7231, FAX: 3-443-7640

Selected Crisp titles are also available in other languages. Contact International Rights Manager Tim Polk at (800) 442-7477 for more information.

Library of Congress Catalog Card Number 92-054365
Rouillard, Larrie
Goals and Goal Setting
ISBN 1-56052-183-X

This book is printed on recyclable paper with soy ink.

ABOUT THIS BOOK

Goals and Goal Setting is not like most books. It has a unique "self-paced" format that encourages a reader to become personally involved. Designed to be "read with a pencil," there is an abundance of exercises, activities, assessments and cases that invite participation.

The objective of this book is to help a person recognize the value of goals and the importance of fundamental goal setting. Completing this book will show how setting and achieving goals can lead to business and personal success.

Goals and Goal Setting (and the other self-improvement books listed in the back of this book) can be used effectively in a number of ways. Here are some possibilities:

- **Individual Study.** Because the book is self-instructional, all that is needed is a quiet place, some time and a pencil. Completing the activities and exercises should provide not only valuable feedback, but also practical ideas about steps for self-improvement.

- **Workshops and Seminars.** This book is ideal for assigned reading prior to a workshop or seminar. With the basics in hand, the quality of participation should improve. More time can be spent on concept extensions and applications during the program. The book is also effective when distributed at the beginning of a session.

- **Remote Location Training.** Copies can be sent to those not able to attend "home office" training sessions.

- **Informal Study Groups.** Thanks to the format, brevity and low cost, this book is ideal for "brown bag" or other informal group sessions.

There are other possibilities that depend on the objectives of the user. One thing for sure, even after it has been read, this book will serve as an excellent reference material which can be easily reviewed. Good luck!

Dedication

To Tina, my purpose and my strength; to Richard and Carolyn, my guides and role models; and to Travis and Brian: may they find an honorable life mission and make their mark through goal achievement.

ABOUT THE AUTHOR

Larrie Rouillard is a business consultant for Safeway, Inc., a Fortune 500 regional retail organization. His specialties include computer systems and regional design, training for retail buying, and merchandising and inventory control applications. He has over 20 years of practical experience in daily business user activities, and has earned two Exceptional Achievement awards for his goal-achieving programs.

Mr. Rouillard is currently assigned as a consultant in northwestern Mexico. He can be contacted through the publisher for comments or questions.

Larrie A. Rouillard

CONTENTS

INTRODUCTION

Achievement and accomplishment are among the more satisfying pleasures human beings experience. Beating the competition to market with a new product, landing that ''big'' account after months of hard work, or finally ridding yourself of a nasty habit are examples of things which people delight in achieving and accomplishing.

Individuals and groups, and self-competitive sports all provide a challenge to succeed—to win. ''Climbing the success ladder'' motivates people to work, inspires creativity, solves problems and stimulates inventiveness to develop new products and ideas.

None of these achievements or accomplishments happens accidently. Achievements and accomplishments are outcomes of a success pattern.

Careful planning, thoughtful strategy and faithful execution are the factors of this pattern. They result *only* when a clear, definable target to aim at exists, and a standard by which to measure progress is available.

Before actions are taken, a goal must exist. The goal is a business or personal purpose or the team's common purpose. The goal is the point that you or the team must reach. Only then can the participant(s) say, ''I've done it!,'' ''We did it!,'' ''We've reached our goal!''

Setting a goal that really motivates is not as easy as it sounds; nor should you think of goal setting as too difficult to be worth your while. A single goal's extraordinary power over the direction of a business is what makes setting a goal very important.

This workbook addresses that important process. The activities in this workbook focus on what a goal is and how to set goals that you can achieve. Step by step, you will practice how to

- Differentiate between goals, missions and objectives
- Use a design for establishing goals
- Construct objectives
- Execute the tactics needed
- Achieve your goals

Your experience tells you that to learn a process you have to practice. You may also realize that learning is easier when you have a purpose. Discovery of the purposes for goals and goal setting is the first step in your learning these new skills.

PURPOSE OF GOAL SETTING

The most obvious question you can ask at this point is "What's in it for me?" If you can't satisfy that question, that is, if you can't recognize your purpose in this learning process, you are not going to be very motivated to do these activities. This discussion of goals and goal setting is separated into topics to make it easier for you to understand what a goal is, and to picture the process needed to set organizational, business and/or personal goals.

Think of the purposes as answers to the questions reporters ask themselves when writing a story:

What? → To identify goals

Why? → To learn the importance of goals and goal setting to business success

Who? → To distinguish the members involved in the goal setting process

Where? → To locate opportunities for useful goals

How? → To effectively reach goals; to accomplish what you want to achieve

The only question missing is "when?" You are the best person to answer that question.

Remember, these objectives are interrelated. They are separated here only for discussion purposes. You have to understand these topics and apply what they require before you can set your goals and achieve them.

Once you understand these purposes, you will see that setting and achieving goals are essential to success in business as well as in life.

Understanding and applying the principles taught in this workbook will provide the foundation for effective goal setting.

WHAT DO YOU THINK?

Look over the following list and mark yes or no in the appropriate column whether you consider the item a goal.

	Yes	No
Increasing sales and profits	☐	☐
Improving productivity in your department	☐	☐
Managing work time more effectively	☐	☐
Seeing the Eiffel Tower in Paris	☐	☐
Capturing the business of an important prospective client	☐	☐
Reducing operating expenses in a critical area in the organization	☐	☐
Being a vice president in your company	☐	☐
Developing a new product within an allotted budget	☐	☐
Learning to play the piano	☐	☐
Gaining market share for your primary product	☐	☐

WHAT DO ALL THESE THINGS HAVE IN COMMON?

In the space below, write what you think are similarities and differences between the items in the list. (*Hint:* They are all things that people have shown can be done).

_____

_____

_____

_____

_____

If you found all of the items on the list are achievable goals, then you might ask yourself questions like these:

"Why can't I . . . ?"

"Why haven't I . . . ?"

"Why don't I . . . ?"

The answer may be that

- You have no real desire to . . . (manage your time more effectively, be a vice-president or do what's necessary to capture that new client).

- If you lack desire to do something, then achieving a GOAL solely for the sake of reaching it will not motivate you enough, nor will you get the same sense of accomplishment.

OR

- You don't know how to establish motivating, stimulating, functional and executable goals.

So, *if* you want to improve department productivity, develop that new product within budget, or just see the Eiffel Tower, *then* you must learn how to set meaningful goals and establish executable objectives that will help you reach those goals.

On the following pages you will find information and activities which survey the basics of goal identification, formulation and execution.

WHY SET GOALS?

Goals are an essential part of successfully conducting business.

Well-defined goals enable choice, design and implementation of important business activities (objectives) necessary to achieve overall desired results (missions).

Goals:
- Establish **DIRECTION** for on-going activities.
- Identify **EXPECTED** results.
- Improve **TEAMWORK** through a common sense of **PURPOSE**.
- Heighten performance levels by setting **TARGETS** to be achieved.

Goals provide the motivation and direction necessary for growth and success in important areas of almost every business. For example:

- *If* you or your company never sets goals for direction, how will your organization know where it is headed?

- *If* no goals exist for progress, how does the organization know where it is?

AND

- *If* there are no goals for achievement, how will the organization know when it has arrived?

Question:

Would you get on an airplane if you didn't know where it was going to land?

P A R T

I

What Is A Goal?

DEFINITION OF A GOAL

Goal—a simple definition:

> *"A GOAL is an end toward which you direct some specific EFFORT."*

In this context the "end" is an exact and tangible result you want and are willing to expend effort to achieve.

What kind of and how much effort is always related to the goal itself, that is, you must be able to identify the cost and benefit relationship. The way you decide if the goal is worth achieving is through planning and analysis of the elements of the goal. Learning how to examine these elements helps you to calculate the cost and benefit relationship.

Elements of a Goal

► An accomplishment to be achieved

"What do I expect the outcome of my (our) actions to be?" In most cases you will want to express this accomplishment with an action word, a verb.

For example: "I want to reduce operating expense in my department from 2% of sales to 1.5%."

► The outcome (accomplishment) is measurable

"How will I know when I have reached the outcome?" "What are the signs I need to see so I know I have reached the goal?" The situation surrounding the accomplishment has to include things you can use to determine you have reached the goal—simple, identifiable signs of success.

For example: "Operating expense was 2% in June, 1.9% in July and is now 1.65% in August. The expenses are heading in the right direction."

DEFINITION OF A GOAL (continued)

► The time factors

"When precisely do I want to have the goal completed?" Just as important as the other elements are a specific date and time by which you will want to be able to say you have accomplished your goal.

For example: "I want to achieve a 1.5% of operating expense to sales by December 1, 1993."

► The cost consideration

"What is the maximum cost (money and resources) I will allow myself to achieve this goal?" "How much will my efforts have cost me when I say 'I've done it'?" The cost and resource constraint forces you to place a financial value on the outcome.

For example: "This reduction in operating expense will be achieved with current headcount and without lowering existing service standards."

The influence of these elements helps to develop the definition of a goal. Below is an expanded definition:

> *"A GOAL is a specific and measurable accomplishment to be achieved within a specified time and under specific cost constraints."*

GOALS MUST BE WRITTEN!

Writing goals in "black and white," gives more explicit statements of intent and results to reach. Daydreaming about your goals does not help you to reach them. Writing your goals out helps you to make sure you have all the elements. It actually the first of several commitments you will make to yourself to reach your goal.

Look at these written goals.

- *"Increase* productivity in our division 5% by August 15, 1993, without adding any personnel."

- *"Gain* five new customers and increase gross sales to $20,000 by July 1, 1993 within an expense budget of $1,000."

- *"Expand* market share to 5% by December 31, 1993 without increasing advertising expense beyond current levels."

- *"Secure* two clients by June 30, 1993 that produce $30,000 income and require only 30% of my time to service."

- *"Celebrate* the 1993 winter holidays in the Barvarian Alps."

You might think the first and last statements have some fuzzy elements to them. Do they have *all* the elements they need to be considered goals? What about the other three?

Reread each goal above and turn the page for some exercises.

EXERCISE #1

Exercise #1

Identify the elements of goal statements in each of the following:

1. Gain five new customers and increase gross sales to $20,000 by July 1, 1993 within an expense budget of $1,000.

   Action verb _____

   Measurable outcome _____

   _____

   Specific date _____

   _____

   Cost constraint _____

   _____

2. Expand market share to 5% by December 31, 1993 without increasing advertising expense beyond current levels.

   Action verb _____

   Measurable outcome _____

   _____

   Specific date _____

   _____

   Cost constraint _____

   _____

3. Secure two clients by June 30, 1993 who will produce $30,000 of income and require no more than 30% of my time to service.

   Action verb _____

   Measurable outcome _____

   _____

   Specific date _____

   _____

   Cost constraint _____

   _____

(Turn to page 80 for answers to Exercise #1)

Exercise #2

With practice, you will learn to easily recognize the elements of a goal. Since you know what the elements of a goal are, you can learn how to write good goals. Start practicing this skill by doing the next exercise.

Write a simple goal using the elements listed on the previous pages.

_____

_____

_____

_____

_____

_____

_____

_____

_____

_____

_____

_____

_____

_____

_____

_____

_____

_____

_____

_____

_____

MISSIONS

One of the purposes of this workbook is to help you distinguish between **goals, missions,** and **objectives.** Now that you know the elements of a goal, you will learn how to use some of those elements to shape missions and objectives. Knowing the differences among these three related types of statements will help you write better statements to achieve your purposes.

Mission—a simple definition:

> *A mission is a general statement through which a person specifies the overall strategy or intent that governs the goals and objectives.*

If a goal is a specific and measurable accomplishment you want to achieve, then a mission is an umbrella statement under which you place your goals and related actions.

A mission statement interprets "reason for being"; it enables you to clarify your purpose for yourself and others who are interested. Some examples of mission statements are

Business:	Improve companywide sales while maintaining expenses and services.
Athletic:	Be a Super Bowl contender.
Personal:	Travel on the European continent.

Examine the examples above carefully and you will notice that a mission statement

- Clearly states the *nature* of your cause.
- Defines your *areas* of concentration.

Do you know your company mission? Write it here.

_____

_____

_____

Having a mission is an important part of the goal-setting process because a mission helps you focus the direction of the goals. For example, if a sports team's mission is,

To be the champion of the National Football League.

then a possible goal could be,

In order to reach the playoffs, beat each team in our division by scoring one touchdown running, one passing, and one field goal in each half while holding opponents scoreless for 60 minutes, all without sustaining any serious injuries.

Note: Goals are complementary to the overall mission. But if there were no mission and no sense of direction, it would be difficult to establish any meaningful goals.

A different mission would require different goals. For example, another mission for an NFL team might read,

It's not whether we win or lose; it's how we play the game.

What are some possible complementary goals for this mission? Write them here.

_____

_____

_____

_____

_____

_____

_____

_____

Now compare your complementary goals and some of the possibilities with the author's example on the next page.

Does your list of goals have the needed elements to distinguish each one from a mission statement?

A COMMENT ABOUT MISSIONS

A possible complementary goal:

Mission:

> *It's not whether we win or lose;*
> *it's how we play the game.*

Complementary Goal:

> *Play all 16 games scheduled without receiving any "unsportsmanlike" or "roughing the passer or kicker" penalties, and without having any players or coaches ejected from a game.*

OBJECTIVES

You have examined the elements needed for goal statements and learned how mission statements use these elements. The next step is to learn how the elements work in establishing *objectives*. Here's how these relationships work:

▶ **Goals** are specific and measurable accomplishments to be achieved.

▶ **Missions** are general intents.

▶ **Objectives** are tactics that you will use to reach and achieve goals.

The objectives and tactics you use must be complementary to the goal, just as goals must be complementary to the mission. For example, if the mission and goals are:

Mission: Be an NFL champion.

Goals: Beat each team in our division.

Then complementary objectives might be

Play Good Defense	• Stop long runs.
	• Intercept a pass.
	• Recover a fumble.
Field Goal	• Control the ball.
	• Get to opponent's 25-yard line.
Passing Game	• Short 12-yard passes.
	• Pass against the weak defender.
Run Game	• Use fullback on short yardage.
	• Run on first down.
	• Run one "reverse" play.

These objectives are the steps to be taken to reach the goal. They determine how fast or slow the goal is reached and what methods will be used to achieve the goal.

GOALS AND OBJECTIVES PYRAMIDS

A pyramid is a good visual illustration of the relationship between missions, goals and objectives. It can also represent the varied approaches used to achieve goals.

The relationship between objectives and goals depends on which approach best satisfies the specific needs for goal achievement and/or personal preference to reaching goals. There are three possible relationships between goals and objectives:

1. Several objectives to achieve one goal

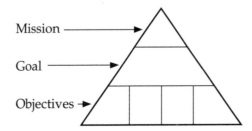

2. One objective to achieve one goal

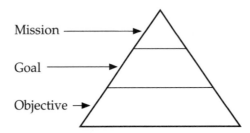

3. Several objectives to achieve several goals

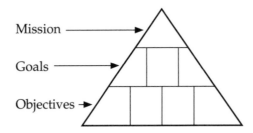

Choosing objectives/tactics that most appropriately fit the desired goals will help you reach the specified goals.

SUMMARY: WHAT IS A GOAL?

> *A goal is an end toward which effort is directed.*

The elements of a goal are

- An *accomplishment* to be achieved

- A *measurable* outcome

- A specific *date* and *time* to accomplish the goal

- A maximum *cost* (money and resources) allowed to achieve the goal

Therefore,

> *A goal is a specific and measurable accomplishment to be achieved within specified time and cost constraints.*

A written goal provides a strong statement of your intent and the results to be achieved. Goal statements contain these elements:

- Action verbs

- Measurable outcomes

- Specific dates and times

- Cost and resource constraints

Mission statements define the cause and outline the overall intent or "reason for being" for an individual, an organization or a business.

Objectives are tactics you use to reach and achieve goals. They must be complementary to the goal and the mission.

P A R T

II

Who Sets Goals and How Do They Agree?

THE PROCESS OF ANALYSIS

Everyone involved in achieving the goal should help set the goal. This is especially true in the business environment. Participation in the goal setting process helps ensure that the goal will be successfully accomplished, because people are more committed to reaching goals they help create. A strictly personal goal requires an internal awareness of the desire and a commitment on the part of the goal setter.

Goal setting should be a negotiation process between the people who are responsible for accomplishing the goal and those who would like to see the goal achieved. The parties involved must agree on the planned accomplishments (goals).

Successful agreement on goals involves a three-step process of analysis that includes discussion, compromise and agreement.

1. Discussion → Presentation of wants, needs and capabilities

2. Compromise → Give-and-take between parties

3. Agreement → Settlement on the goals to be achieved

THE THREE-STEP PROCESS

Discussion

The discussion step involves getting all the interested parties together to discuss the who, what, when, why, where, how and how much of the desired goal, as well as the expected outcome.

In this step, data and details of the goal are openly discussed so that everyone involved clearly understands the intent and purpose of the goal. Everyone involved must feel comfortable with the why, what, how and how much of the detailed goal before committing to goal achievement.

Once all the elements are openly discussed, areas of agreement and disagreement will be exposed so that the parties can proceed to the next step—compromise.

Compromise

Goal setting requires that negotiation reaches a compromise before goals can be achieved. The compromise will determine who, what, when, how and how much will be done to achieve the GOAL. There must be give-and-take between the parties that want the goal achieved and those that will be responsible for achieving the goal.

Compromise is an essential part of goal achievement because it establishes the goal boundaries, the elements of the goal to be executed and the expected results to be accomplished. Compromise is necessary for reaching agreement.

Agreement

Agreement closes out the compromise step and sets the ground rules for goal execution and the efforts to be expended for goal achievement. Everyone involved must agree on the costs (money and resources) and benefits (hard and soft), as well as the methods to be used to achieve the goal.

Without agreement on a united and concerted effort by everyone involved, the goal may not be reached. Discussion, compromise and agreement require that people interact with one another during the goal-setting process. Because this interaction means that people must talk, the most essential element in the early stages of goal setting is

Communication

COMMUNICATION

Communication is the result of your efforts to let other people know what is going on. Communication is critical because goals will be difficult to achieve unless all levels of the organization clearly understand the mission and the goals.

Since everyone doesn't see or hear everything in exactly the same way, deliberate communication actions expand the chances that everyone involved will understand the goals and direction (mission). Understanding ensures success.

Communication is crucial for

► Getting individuals to accept goals

► Using goals to manage progress

► Assigning and assuming responsibility for reaching difficult goals

Within the context of who sets the goal, it is also important to consider how the goal will be established.

There are two general approaches to who sets the goal in the goal setting process:

- *Top-down goal setting:* Management sets the goal for lower levels to achieve.

- *Bottom-up goal setting:* Individuals at lower levels commit to performance they can achieve.

GOAL SETTING FROM THE TOP DOWN

TOP-DOWN GOAL SETTING

Top-down goal setting reflects the needs of the organization as a whole (the need for sales and profitability, customers' needs, and so on). These needs dictate the contribution required by lower levels to achieve the goal.

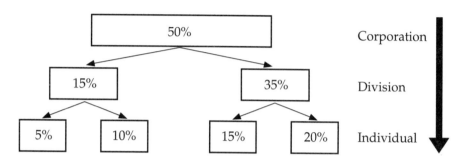

In the previous example, the corporation's goal is to achieve a 50% increase. This increase will come from the two divisions at the lower level, split 35% and 15% respectively.

The 35% division will achieve its goal by getting a 15% increase from one individual, and a 20% increase from the other.

The 15% division requires a 5% and 10% contribution from its individuals.

The 50% GOAL established for the company drives the contribution needs of the lower levels.

Question: What are the dangers of top-down goal setting in the business environment?

Write your answer here and then compare your thoughts with the author's on page 82.

_____

_____

_____

_____

_____

_____

BOTTOM-UP GOAL SETTING

Although it is frequently more time-consuming and difficult to do, bottom-up goal setting is preferable. It confirms the skills and potential contributions of employees at lower levels to the organization as a whole. It puts goal setting at the level where the product is made or where the services are done.

Organizations that involve all levels of employees in the planning of goals and objectives to achieve the corporate mission usually achieve more because most everyone has a stake in the commitments.

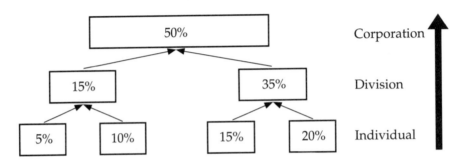

In this scenario, each individual commits to the share he or she is capable of contributing. In this case, the four individuals can each contribute 5%, 10%, 15%, and 20% respectively to the next level.

This commitment allows the two divisions to commit to a 15% and 35% share to the corporation goal of a 50% increase.

Question: What are the dangers of bottom-up goal setting in the business environment?

Write your answer here and then compare your thoughts with the author's on page 82.

_____

_____

_____

_____

_____

_____

_____

PART

III

How Are Goals Set?

A FOUR-TASK PROCESS

Goals evolve from a discovery process in which you identify a problem, dream about a potential innovation, or review the essential aspects of your job or life to find accomplishments that you want to achieve.

When you uncover the Who? What? When? How? and How much? of a particular activity, you have the raw material for goal setting.

Goal setting is a sequence of events that enables the creation of attainable, actionable, and rewarding goals that lead to positive results.

Creating goals is a four-task process:

Task 1: Identify opportunities for goals.

Task 2: Write goal statements.

Task 3: Develop goals.

Task 4: Formulate action plans.

The pages that follow describe each of these goal-setting tasks.

TASK 1: IDENTIFY OPPORTUNITIES FOR GOALS

Questions:	Where are specific goals found?
	Where does an organization or individual find the best opportunities for creating goals?
Answer:	All around you and the organization!

Opportunities can be found in your personal life or in your business life. Goals can be anything associated with your business or personal life so long as they contribute to an organizational or individual mission (reason for being).

Find goals for the organization or the individual within the organization itself. Consider both internal and external factors as opportunities for goal creation.

Personal Desires

Goals develop from ''seeds'': ideas, wants, needs and desires. Each seed can produce many individual goals. For example, a *personal* desire might be,

I would like to learn a foreign language so that I can travel to different parts of the world and experience new cultures.

This one desire contains the seeds for many possible goals:

1. Learn a foreign language.
2. Travel to other parts of the world.
3. Experience new cultures.

These desires can be transformed into a goal statement that leads to achievement of the goal itself. For example,

I will enroll in a six-month foreign language course by March 31, 1993 and become proficient enough in the language to carry on a conversation within one year.

or

I will make reservations to travel to _____ by March 31, 1993 at a cost not to exceed $_____.

TASK 1: IDENTIFY OPPORTUNITES FOR GOALS (continued)

Each of these goal statements provides the material necessary for shaping additional objectives and formulating plans to achieve the goal.

Write a personal desire here.

_____

_____

_____

_____

_____

_____

_____

_____

_____

_____

What are some of the potential "seeds" for goals that you can develop from this personal desire?

1. _____

_____

2. _____

_____

3. _____

_____

4. _____

_____

Business Desires

A *business* desire might be,

I would like to have enough sales and profit to be able to have my own truck fleet and quit relying on other truckers for my deliveries.

Again, this one statement has numerous potential goals that could be acted upon. For example,

1. Increase sales
2. Increase profits
3. Improve delivery service
4. Purchase own truck fleet

Each idea can become a distinct goal statement.

Increase sales by 5% per quarter for the next year ending March 31, 1993 by developing new clients from outside our current market area without adding any additional salespeople.

or

Purchase one new truck every six months beginning April 1, 1993 by using increased sales to finance the truck cost, a cost not to exceed 1% of the net sales increase.

Write a business desire here.

_____

_____

_____

_____

_____

_____

_____

TASK 1: IDENTIFY OPPORTUNITES FOR GOALS (continued)

What are some of the potential goals you can develop from this business desire?

1. _____

_____

2. _____

_____

3. _____

_____

4. _____

_____

Goals are meant to establish direction for a business or an individual. They provide a firm foundation for building a set of tactics (objectives) necessary to accomplish the goal.

GOALS: YOUR ULTIMATE DESTINATION

GOAL IDENTIFICATION VS. GOAL DEVELOPMENT

In the goal identification phase, it's not important to establish all the details involved with goal achievement or to determine the exact objectives needed to succeed. Those elements are part of goal development (discussed later).

The object of this phase is to identify where an individual or business wants to be in one, two, or five years. The primary objective of goal identification is to give substance to what would otherwise only be dreams and desires.

Goals are destinations that not only survey where the business or the individual has been and is now, but they also combine relevant knowledge with dreams and desires to set a direction for the future.

Focus your attention on the ultimate destination. Objectives or milestones are only steps toward the goal. The specific objectives may change as progress toward the goal is made, but the goal itself, once it is established, should remain unchanged. For example,

> If the mission is to "experience many different cultures" and the goal is "to travel around the world," then the various destinations (objectives) may change because of travel constraints, the desire to see places not on the original itinerary or expense, but the original goal—to travel around the world—will not change.

On the lines below, write down one personal goal that you want to achieve in the next two years.

_____

_____

Now list three objectives that you will use to identify that you are making progress toward your goal.

1. _____

   _____

2. _____

   _____

3. _____

   _____

GOAL TYPES

When you are identifying goals, it is helpful to categorize different goals by type. This clarifies their importance to the mission. There are three types of goals, each of which differ in the contribution they make to the declared mission:

► **Essential goals** are necessary for continued, ongoing progress.

► **Problem-solving goals** propose a more appropriate or desired condition.

► **Innovative goals** make something good even better.

When you understand goal types, you will be able to identify the possible opportunities that are all around, and you will be able to determine the relative importance of the opportunity to the individual or the organization.

Let's investigate goal types in more detail.

Essential Goals

An essential goal identifies everyday activities that require improvement and must be fulfilled to ensure successful results. Essential goals are the recurring, ongoing, repetitious and necessary activities of business or personal life. These activities are essential to ongoing success. For example,

Review yesterday's results by 9:00 a.m., and correct errors before new work begins.

Can you think of an essential goal that you must accomplish on a regular basis? (*Hint:* ''Getting up on time tomorrow'' may be part of an essential goal, if it's to ensure you'll be on time for an important meeting.) Write it here.

_____

_____

_____

Sources of essential goals can usually be found in one's area of responsibility.

Assess the tasks you're responsible for to uncover those elements that must be dealt with on a regular basis. For example, if your area of responsibility is sorting the mail, then you must set goals for specific activities such as: efficient mail sorting, timing considerations and effective delivery routes. The key is,

Essential goals are those that must get accomplished on a routine basis.

Problem-Solving Goals

A problem-solving goal identifies a current problem or opportunity along with a more appropriate or desired condition. It is a statement of a current and future situation once a solution is implemented.

Problem-solving goals outline the activities necessary to improve performance. They are vital to growth, but may not be detrimental if not accomplished. For example,

> *Reduce the number of mismatched invoices from 50% to 20% of the invoices received by the end of the 4th quarter, 1993, with no additions to head count.*

This statement outlines the problem (50% mismatches in invoices received), and the more appropriate or desired condition (only 20% mismatches) that needs to be achieved.

Can you think of a problem-solving goal that ought to be accomplished? Write it here.

_____

_____

_____

_____

_____

Sources for problem-solving goals are

- Aspects of the task that can be improved, such as productivity, efficiency, accident prevention.

- Less-than-effective use of time or resources.

- Obstacles in the workplace that can be eliminated.

Ask yourself: What's involved in solving these problems? The answer to this question can provide the seeds for developing problem-solving goals.

Innovative Goals

An innovative goal improves the current condition. Innovative goals are not problems, but rather the result of thinking about making something good even better. They identify activities to be done better, faster, cheaper, easier or more safely. For example,

> *Introduce a change to the existing computer-buying system that will reduce the number of hours needed to determine promotional quantities by the end of the 2nd quarter, 1993, using existing programs to keep development costs below $10,000.*

This statement says that there may be nothing at all wrong with the current condition, but that if improvements could be made, then the system would be better and promotional quantities could be determined more easily than before.

Create an innovative goal that would be nice to do, and write it here.

_____

_____

Innovative goals are sometimes the more pleasurable type of goals to create because they represent our dreams more than our needs.

Other Potential Areas

Many other aspects of business or personal life can provide opportunities for goal creation. For example:

▶ *Profitability.* Increasing profitability may require essential, problem-solving or innovative goals to maintain or obtain higher yields from existing sources. Focus on profitability from two perspectives: cost control and higher prices. Both will yield more profit, therefore profitability provides two different elements for potential goals.

▶ *Self-improvement.* Self-improvement may mean finding additional areas of interest, or new responsibilities to be added over the course of a career. These are personal goals that you may want to accomplish in one year, two years, or five years from now. Setting intermediary essential or innovative goals can help you attain these personal goals.

▶ *Market conditions.* Analyze the needs of your market area to create problem-solving or innovative goals. Analyze customer needs, uncover market weaknesses and identify market advantages. Develop goals from the limits of each type.

TASK 1: SUMMARY

✔ Goals can be anything so long as they contribute to the mission (reason for being) of the individual, the business or the organization.

✔ Goals identify the direction of the organization or individual; they are the ultimate "destinations" of our dreams, needs and desires.

✔ Goals are developed from ideas, wants, needs and desires. They can come from our business or our personal lives.

✔ Goals should not change once they are set. However, objectives to reaching goals can and should change as conditions change.

✔ Essential goals must be accomplished for the success of the organization or the individual.

✔ Problem-solving goals ought to be done to correct ineffective conditions and thereby produce better results.

✔ Innovative goals are those we would like to do in order to make something good even better (faster, cheaper, safer or easier).

Essential goals should not be passed over to achieve the relatively less important problem-solving or innovative goals. Innovative or problem-solving goals should not jeopardize your ability to achieve essential goals.

Try to find opportunities to achieve multiple goals by completing objectives that are common to two or more goals. Obviously, this requires careful planning and written statements that you can mix and match as needed.

Goal Setting in Practice:
Task 1

Remember: The purpose of the identification task is solely to uncover the wants, needs and desires for future personal or business accomplishments.

Personal desire: "I would like to learn a foreign language so that I can travel to different parts of the world and experience new cultures."

Possible goal "seeds": Learn the French language.
Travel to France and experience French culture.
See the Eiffel Tower.

Goal type: *Innovative*—Nice to do. "It would be nice to know how to speak French while traveling in France. My travel would be much easier if I knew the language."

Goal objective: Self-improvement.

TASK 2: WRITING GOAL STATEMENTS

A well-defined goal statement is the foundation for goal achievement. The goal is only as good as its statement of desire and intent to

- Fulfill one's responsibilities

- Solve a problem

- Be creative and innovative

- Have a better business or personal life

A goal statement formalizes

What is to be accomplished

Who will be involved

When the activity will be completed

How much cost and resources will be used

The "S.M.A.R.T." way to ensure all these elements of a well-defined goal are included in each goal statement. The S.M.A.R.T. goal statement is

SPECIFIC

MEASURABLE

ACTION-ORIENTED

REALISTIC

TIME- AND RESOURCE-CONSTRAINED

A goal statement that contains each of these elements will provide an excellent basis for setting and monitoring progress and achieving the goal.

S.M.A.R.T. GOALS ARE SPECIFIC

Specific means detailed, particular or focused. A goal is specific when everyone knows exactly what is to be achieved and accomplished. Being specific means spelling out the details of the goal. For example:

> ''Increase productivity'' is too general for a goal statement because it does not provide any specific information about what is to be accomplished.

> ''Increase the secretarial typing pool productivity . . .'' is more specific because it narrows the scope of the desired outcome.

But to be the most specific, a goal statement should say something like,

> *Increase the letter-typing output (productivity) of the secretarial pool . . .*

This last statement specifies the desired improvement and leaves no doubt about what is to be accomplished.

Specifying the expected end result is the first step toward creating a S.M.A.R.T. goal.

EXERCISE #3

Exercise #3

Rate the following statements. Are they specific enough to spell out the details of the desired goal? After you complete this exercise, check your answers on page 80.

	Too General	Not Specific Enough	More Specific
A. Wash and clean the car.	☐	☐	☐
B. Wash and clean the car each week.	☐	☐	☐
C. Wash and clean the car inside and out each week.	☐	☐	☐
D. Get better grades in school.	☐	☐	☐
E. Get better math grades in school.	☐	☐	☐
F. Get at least a B in math in school each semester.	☐	☐	☐
G. Study more often.	☐	☐	☐
H. Study my assignments every day.	☐	☐	☐
I. Study my math assignments at least one hour each day.	☐	☐	☐

Write an example of a *specific* end result.

_____

_____

_____

_____

S.M.A.R.T. GOALS ARE MEASURABLE

Measurable goals are quantifiable. A measurable goal provides a standard for comparison, the means to an end, a specific result; it is limiting. Each goal must be measurable—it must have a method for comparison that indicates when the goal is reached. Doing something "better," or "more accurately," or even "precisely" does not provide the quantifiable measurement necessary to determine goal achievement. These words are too ambiguous for a measurable outcome. For example,

> "Increase the letter-typing output of the secretarial pool . . ." is a *specific* statement, but to be measurable, it needs the addition of ". . . to 40 completed letters per day."

The words "40 completed letters per day" provide a standard for comparison and progress measurement.

Counting the completed letter output each day will indicate when and where progress is made toward the goal, and will determine when the 40-letters-per-day goal is reached; this provides a measurable limit for the goal.

Exercise #4

Check *Yes* or *No* to indicate whether each of the following is a *measurable* outcome. After you complete this exercise, check your answers on page 80.

	Yes	No
A. Provide better service to all my customers.	☐	☐
B. Answer every letter received within five work days.	☐	☐
C. Significantly reduce the number of complaints.	☐	☐
D. Lower the number of complaints by 50% of current levels.	☐	☐
E. Add only very productive individuals to the staff.	☐	☐

Remember: Measurable statements must be quantifiable, a standard for comparison, and limiting.

Write a *measurable* statement here.

_____

_____

_____

S.M.A.R.T. GOALS ARE ACTION-ORIENTED

Action-oriented means that the goal statements indicate an activity, a performance, an operation or something that produces results. Action-oriented goal statements tell what is to be done to reach the goal. This action is indicated by use of an action verb. Action verbs describe the type of activity to be performed. Here are some examples of action verbs:

evaluate	*investigate*
appraise	*influence*
inform	*restrict*

For example, in the statement,

"Increase the letter output," the verb "increase" indicates that the expected result is to raise the productivity from the existing level to a more desirable level.

What are some other action-oriented verbs that indicate expected performance?

_____   _____   _____

_____   _____   _____

_____   _____   _____

S.M.A.R.T. GOALS ARE REALISTIC

Realistic goals are practical, achievable and possible. Goals must motivate people to improve and to reach for attainable ends. For a goal to be motivational, the goal-seeker must feel that the goal can be achieved ("I can do it!"). This realization must occur before effort and energy are applied toward reaching the goal. For example,

> "Increasing the secretarial pool output to 40 completed letters per day" is possible and achievable (realistic) only if the current level of output is 23–30 letters per day. If the current level is only 4 completed letters per day, the "40 completed letters per day" may not be realistic with the existing staff.

The goal is practical only if a need exists to achieve the goal. For example,

> *if there are no more than 10 letters that need to be typed each day, setting a 40 letter GOAL is unnecessary.*

Impossible goals demotivate and defeat the goal-setting process. No one strives for goals that cannot be reached. Goals should not be too easy, either. Easy goals do not motivate any more than unattainable goals.

Realistic goals are a balance between what is hard and what is easy to achieve. They require a "stretch" that reaches beyond what is easily achieved and establishes a more challenging goal. It's that little bit extra in performance that makes people progress and improve. "Stretching" creates the necessary balance between the effort required to achieve the goal, and the probability of success.

> *Challenging, realistic goals motivate and encourage higher levels of performance.*

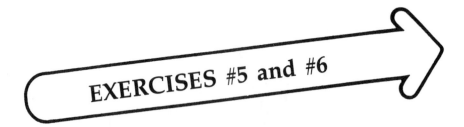
EXERCISES #5 and #6

Exercise #5

Realistic goals are practical, achievable and possible. Are the following goal components realistic?

	Realistic	Unrealistic
A. Swim a mile.	☐	☐
B. Swim across the Pacific Ocean.	☐	☐
C. Hold your breath until you faint.	☐	☐
D. Learn to play the piano in one year.	☐	☐

Exercise #6

How does the "stretch" principle apply to a short-distance runner who would like to become a marathoner?

_____

_____

_____

_____

_____

_____

_____

_____

_____

(Check your answers with those of the author's on page 81.)

S.M.A.R.T. GOALS ARE TIME- AND RESOURCE-CONSTRAINED

Time- and resource-constrained means scheduled; regulated by time and resources to be expended; a finite duration to the action allowed; a deadline. People generally put off doing things if no deadline is set because human nature always finds something else to do that has a higher priority.

Time constraints encourage action to get activities completed. Deadlines encourage activity. For example, a time- and resource-constrained goal statement might be,

> *Increase the letter-typing output of the secretarial pool to 40 completed letters per day by June 30, 1993, without adding any new typists.''*

The precise date provides a deadline, while the "without adding any new typists" places a limit on the resources to use to achieve the goal.

Time constraints and deadlines must be precise to promote the urgency needed to move toward goal achievement. For example,

> "By the end of October" is more specific than "toward the end of October." But it is not as precise as, "by 10:00 a.m. on October 31, 1993." This deadline leaves no doubt about when the goal should be achieved.

Some goals are easily achievable when money and resources are unlimited. We spend until the goal is reached. For example,

> One way of achieving the "40 letters per day goal" is to have 40 typists available. That assures one typist for each desired letter. In the real world, however, money and resources are constraints that must be considered in most businesses.

The goal statement must contain resource constraints in order to ensure that there is a practical cost/benefit relationship to goal achievement.

EXERCISE #7

Exercise #7

Which of the following phrases represent deadlines, and which are just expressions of time?

	Deadline?	
	Yes	No
A. Next week	☐	☐
B. Next Thursday by noon	☐	☐
C. As soon as possible	☐	☐
D. First thing Monday morning	☐	☐
E. Before the close of business today	☐	☐
F. Before the close of business today, at 5:00 p.m. PST	☐	☐
G. December 31, 1999	☐	☐

Write your own *precise deadlines* below.

_____

_____

_____

_____

(Check your answers with those of the author's on page 81.)

TASK 2: SUMMARY

S.M.A.R.T. goals ensure that all the necessary elements are included for creating actionable, well-planned and achievable goals. The S.M.A.R.T. goal is

SPECIFIC

✔ Detailed, particular, focused

✔ ''Increase the letter typing output of the secretarial pool . . .''

MEASURABLE

✔ Quantifiable, a standard for comparison, the means to a specific result, limiting

✔ '' . . . to 40 completed letters per day.''

ACTION-ORIENTED

✔ Performing, operating, producing results

✔ ''Increase . . . completed . . . ''

REALISTIC

✔ Practical, achievable, accurate, possible

✔ ''(Increase) . . . from current level (20–30 per day) to 40 completed letters per day''

TIME- AND RESOURCE-CONSTRAINED

✔ Scheduled, regulated by time, a finite duration of activity, extent of resources allowed, deadline

✔ ''By June 30, 1993, without adding any new typists''

Goal Setting in Practice:
Task 2

Remember: The goal statement is a very important part of goal achievement because it lays the foundation for goal development and execution.

Goal statements must be S.M.A.R.T. . . . .

SPECIFIC
MEASURABLE
ACTION-ORIENTED
REALISTIC
TIME- AND RESOURCE-CONSTRAINED

Personal desire: ''I would like to learn a foreign language so that I can travel to different parts of the world and experience new cultures.''

Possible goal statement: ''Learn the French language with sufficient fluency to be able to carry on a complete conversation with a fluent friend or a French teacher by December 31, 1993, one year and six months from now, within a cost not to exceed $3000 for books, materials, and courses.''

Specific: ''Learn the French language''

Measurable: ''Sufficient fluency to be able to carry on a complete conversation with a fluent friend''

Action-oriented: ''Learn . . . carry on a conversation''

Realistic: Languages can be learned in an 18-month period with appropriate training and study.

Time- and resource-constrained: December 31, 1993 deadline; cost constraint of $3000.

TASK 3: DEVELOP GOALS

Identifying opportunities (Task 1), and creating S.M.A.R.T. goal statements (Task 2) are two essential elements needed to complete Task 3, goal development.

Goal development expands goal statements to provide context and substance for expected results and benefits. It identifies the importance, effort, benefits and results of each goal statement created.

Completion of Task 1 (Identify . . .) and Task 2 (Goal statements) may result in one, two, ten or fifty legitimate goal statements that will require development (Task 3) before the necessary activities toward goal achievement can begin.

You should complete goal development for every legitimate goal statement created. There are five steps to effective goal development:

1. Classify goals by type.

2. Prioritize within each type.

3. Establish standards of performance.

4. Identify obstacles to goal achievement.

5. Determine ''W.I.I.F.M.'' (What's In It For Me?).

Each of these important and necessary steps to goal development is described in the following pages.

CLASSIFY GOALS BY TYPE

The classification of goals requires a review of each goal statement to determine whether the end result (accomplishment to be achieved) is:

- *Essential* — it is required for the operation of the business, or for personal improvement. It *must* be done.

- *Problem-solving* — it identifies a less-than-ideal condition and a proposed solution that ought to be done.

- *Innovative* — it is a nice-to-be-done activity that will result in something better, faster, cheaper, easier or safer.

To classify your goals, create a list of goal statements for each goal type.

Essential goals	→	Essential goal A Essential goal B Essential goal C, etc.
Problem-solving goals	→	Problem-solving goal A Problem-solving goal B Problem-solving goal C, etc.
Innovative goals	→	Innovative goal A Innovative goal B Innovative goal C, etc.

This provides a workable list of identified goals to be achieved.

Goal statements may overlap into multiple types. For example, a possible overlapping goal statement might be:

Learn the French language with sufficient fluency to be able to carry on a complete conversation with a fluent friend and be able to translate the French instruction materials received with the machinery used in the production plant.

CLASSIFY GOALS BY TYPE (continued)

This innovative goal to learn French takes on an additional problem-solving motive if knowing French would solve your company's problem of needing a French translator to translate materials each time a new machine is received from the French manufacturer. One motive is purely self-improvement, while accomplishing the goal also solves a business problem.

When this occurs, you need to classify overlapping statements by the highest level of need.

Goal Type	Level of Need
Essential	Must be done
Problem-solving	Ought to be done
Innovative	Nice to be done

For example, a combination essential and problem-solving goal should be classified as an essential goal because it must be done, and therefore has the highest level of need.

Likewise, an essential/innovative goal is classified as an essential goal. A problem-solving/innovative goal would be included in the problem-solving list because ''ought to be done'' is a more critical need than ''nice to be done.''

The key to the correct classification of goal statements is to remember that some goals *must be done*, while others *ought to be done*, and still others would be *nice to be done*.

PRIORITIZE GOALS WITHIN TYPE

The next step in goal development is to determine the most significant goal to be achieved within each type. Setting priorities results in a list of goals that ensures that the most important goal will be acted on first.

Prioritize the essential goals first, followed by the problem-solving goals, and finally the innovative goals, as illustrated below:

			Assigned Priority
Essential goals	→	Essential goal A	_____
		Essential goal B	_____
		Essential goal C, etc.	_____
Problem-solving goals	→	Problem-solving goal A	_____
		Problem-solving goal B	_____
		Problem-solving goal C, etc.	_____
Innovative goals	→	Innovative goal A	_____
		Innovative goal B	_____
		Innovative goal C, etc.	_____

Here are some examples of criteria for setting priorities:

► *Relative importance:* The achievement of essential goal B is objectively more important to the company (or to me) than achieving either essential goals A or C.

► *Time sequence:* Essential goals A and C cannot be achieved until essential goal B is completed, therefore B must have the highest priority.

► *Cost-benefit relationship:* Essential goal B can be achieved at a lower cost than either A or C and will produce immediate benefits. Therefore, B should have the highest essential goal priority.

PRIORITIZE GOALS WITHIN TYPE (continued)

Other objective criteria can be used as well to establish priority within goal types. The key is to establish criteria within each type. There should be no problem-solving goals with a higher priority than the *lowest* essential goal.

If a problem-solving goal (ought to be done) appears to warrant a priority higher than the lowest essential goal (must be done), then one or the other goal statement may be classified incorrectly. Carefully review each goal statement to ensure that a correct classification has been assigned.

Prioritizing is simplified when you have created very specific goal statements. Specific goal statements include *what* is to be accomplished and *why*, along with the expected beneficial results (must be, ought to be, nice to be) and the cost and resource constraints allowed.

This information provides everything necessary to make a judgement on the classification and priority of the goal.

ESTABLISH STANDARDS FOR PERFORMANCE

The next necessary step in goal development is to identify a standard for performance that indicates the level of results expected for each goal. Standards of performance serve two purposes. They

1. Indicate progress made toward the goal.
2. Tell when the goal has been achieved.

It is important that these standards be established *before* any activities begin. They represent specific objectives or milestones to be reached during progress toward goals. Specific times must be established to indicate when progress will be measured—in future days, weeks, months or years.

Three separate standards for performance should be established:

► *Minimal:* Indicates that some progress has been made toward goal achievement, but may not be at a pace sufficient to guarantee goal achievement.

► *Acceptable:* Progress made is consistent with goal achievement during the time allotted.

► *Outstanding:* More progress than expected was achieved when measured at the milestone date.

For example, if the goal is,

Increase secretarial pool letter output from 24 letters completed per day to 40 letters per day, by October 31, 1993, (six months from now).

Then standards for performance might be

26 letters completed within 3 months = MINIMAL
31 letters completed within 3 months = ACCEPTABLE
34 letters completed within 3 months = OUTSTANDING

or

32 letters completed within 5 months = MINIMAL
35 letters completed within 5 months = ACCEPTABLE
38 letters completed within 5 months = OUTSTANDING

Remember, standards of performance that serve as objectives will indicate progress by specifying

• *When* improvement is expected.

• *What* the situation will be after it is improved.

Proper standards for comparison include a time element for review (''within three months'') and a quantifiable standard for progress (''34 letters per day'').

IDENTIFY OBSTACLES TO GOAL ACHIEVEMENT

There may be obstacles that block the way to goal achievement. Goals can be blocked by physical, conditional or psychological obstacles that must be overcome in order to reach the goal.

Each type of obstacle is a real barrier to goal achievement. It makes no difference if the barrier is tangible (physical or conditional), or solely in one's own mind (psychological)—the barrier is *real*. Therefore, it is very important to

1. Identify the obstacle to achievement of the goal.

2. Plan a way to overcome the obstacle.

Often there are many obstacles to individual goals. It is necessary to identify every possible and conceivable obstacle in order to develop a complete and comprehensive plan for overcoming them and drawing closer to the goal.

Physical Obstacles

Physical obstacles are blocks beyond the immediate control of the individual. These obstacles may make it appear impossible to achieve the goal. For example, physical obstacles that block the goal to

Increase the secretarial pool letter output to 40 completed letters per day . . .

might be

The word processing system becomes inoperative and will not function for an extended period of time.

This is a potential block to goal achievement. Buying, installing and retraining employees in the use of a new word processing system could have a serious impact on the time schedule for goal achievement.

It is important to anticipate this possibility and have a plan of action ready if this situation occurs; when you are prepared to take the actions necessary, you will avoid a major block to goal achievement.

What possible steps could be planned to overcome the physical obstacle of a new word processing system so that progress toward goal achievement can continue?

Write your thoughts here and check them with the thoughts of the author (page 83).

_____

_____

_____

_____

_____

_____

Planning for these possibilities may mean the difference between abandoning the goal and achieving the goal.

Changing Objectives

What changes to the objectives should be considered?

_____

_____

_____

_____

_____

Physical obstacles may be very difficult to overcome because these barriers are real obstacles to the goal itself. Planning for them helps you avoid surprises that can sink goals.

(See author's comments on page 83.)

Conditional Obstacles

Conditional obstacles are those where current conditions exist that may make it difficult to attain the goal. For example,

> *How can we meet our goal of 40 letters per day while learning a new word processing system?*

In this scenario, the conditional block is that two tasks need to be performed at the same time (one planned for goal achievement, and another spontaneous but also important task).

Once again, anticipation and proper planning can help ensure that both tasks can be accomplished. Contingency plans are needed to avoid surprise conditions that can impact goal achievement.

What possible actions could be taken to overcome the above conditional obstacle to goal achievement?

_____

_____

_____

_____

_____

_____

_____

_____

_____

_____

Conditional obstacles may be the easiest type to overcome, because they may only require establishing new objectives or tactics that bypass the obstacle.

(See author's comments on page 83.)

Psychological Obstacles

Psychological obstacles are those that exist only in one's own mind. They can be self-confidence issues that block advancement toward the goal. One must believe that the goal can be achieved. If there is doubt about the possibility of achieving the goal, a psychological obstacle is created.

Psychological obstacles are no less intimidating than the more tangible physical or conditional obstacles. They present a real roadblock to the goal seeker.

Psychological obstacles are sometimes the most difficult to overcome because they poison one's mind. For example, the head of the secretarial pool might think,

> *Typing 40 completed letters per day is impossible. . . . We'll never reach that goal.*

This kind of thought process is self-defeating and keeps people from starting the goal achievement process. (If you don't start, you can never finish!)

What methods can help overcome psychological obstacles?

1. _____

_____

_____

2. _____

_____

_____

3. _____

_____

_____

(*Check the author's thoughts on page 83.*)

UNPRODUCTIVE ACTIVITIES

The most dangerous obstacle to goal achievement is unproductive activities. This obstacle is a form of procrastination, but it is more dangerous because it is harder to detect than procrastination.

Unproductive activities appear to be relevant to goal accomplishment, but in fact they do not actually help achieve the goal. For example:

- Researching and reviewing word-processing software packages beyond the point of satisfaction, then waiting until the chosen system is available and installed before beginning to execute planned objectives.

- Interviewing to hire every typist needed before starting the existing typists on goal achievement activities.

- Taking everyone on a field trip to view an office that *does* achieve an output of 40 letters per day.

Each of these may be very good and necessary activities and may need to be part of the overall plan for goal achievement. However, they do not directly contribute to goal achievement.

The only activities that are relevant are those included as objectives in the goal-achievement planning process. Simply doing something every day gives the appearance of performing activity toward reaching the goal. However, unless the individual is truly focused on the goal itself (not just on any activity), the time and resources invested may be wasted. The effort may not be directed toward the specific, established goal.

Methods for avoiding unproductive activities include

▶ Establishing clear, focused goal statements.

▶ Performing only those activities that meet objectives and that result in goal achievement.

▶ Continually reviewing the results, priorities and plans that lead to established goals.

DETERMINE W.I.I.F.M.
(WHAT'S IN IT FOR ME?)

One critical element for success is determining, "What's in it for me?" "How do I directly benefit from achieving this goal?" People who are committed to achieving goals that they helped create are even more committed to goals that benefit them personally, even in a business environment.

Monetary incentives, recognition, pride and self-improvement are all good motivators. People perform better when they are convinced that there are personal benefits that can result by accomplishing a goal.

When you develop business goals, it's important to identify any personal advantages or benefits as well. For personal goals, you must first convince *yourself* of the benefits if you expect to adequately perform the tasks necessary for goal achievement. For example:

Goal	W.I.I.F.M.
Lose those last 10 pounds.	I'll get to wear all those clothes that don't fit now.
Learn a new PC software program.	I can do my current job faster and it will make me more promotable in the future.

Commitment to goal achievement sometimes means looking at the goal from a more selfish perspective.

TASK 3: SUMMARY

There are five important steps in goal development:

1. **Classify goals by type:**
  - Essential: Must be done
  - Problem-solving: Ought to be done
  - Innovative: Nice to be done

2. **Prioritize your goals:**
  - Essential goals are more important than . . .
  - Problem-solving goals, which are more important than . . .
  - Innovative goals

Rank goals within each category based on *relative importance, time sequence, and cost/benefit relationship.*

3. **Establish standards of performance that include:**
  - An established time for review of progress
  - A quantitative method for determining progress:
    —Minimal: Some progress
    —Acceptable: Enough progress
    —Outstanding: More than expected progress

4. **Identify all obstacles to goal achievement:**

Formulate contingency plans for overcoming potential physical, conditional, or psychological obstacles.

5. **Determine W.I.I.F.M. (What's In It For Me?)**

There must *always* be a personal motive identified to ensure motivation toward goal achievement, especially in the business environment.

Goal Setting in Practice:
Task 3

Remember: Goal development expands the goal statement to provide context and substance for the expected results and benefits. Let's demonstrate the five steps in goal development.

Goal statement: *Learn the French language with sufficient fluency to be able to carry on a complete conversation with a fluent friend or a French teacher by December 31, 1993, one year and six months from now, within a cost for books, materials, and courses not to exceed $3000.*

1. *Classify:* Innovative, Nice-to-Do. "There is no pressure to learn French. I want to learn the language in order to make it easier to travel in France and visit the Eiffel Tower."

2. *Prioritize:* "I cannot quit my job to study French full time; therefore, my first priority is my job. However, in terms of my free time, I would like to give this a very high priority. I am willing to devote two or three nights per week to formal French classes."

3. *Standards of Performance:* "If I take French classes at least two nights per week, after three months, I should be able to listen to and understand at least 50 percent of a conversation by other students.

   "After six months, I should understand 90 percent of what is said and participate somewhat in the conversation.

   "After one year, I should be able to understand a conversation totally and fully participate in a discussion with other students.

   "After 18 months, I will converse fluently with the teacher or a native of France with little difficulty."

Goal Setting in Practice (continued)

Goal statement
(continued):

4. *Obstacles:*

PHYSICAL OBSTACLE: Finding an effective training or school.

HOW TO OVERCOME: Seek out references and conduct an investigation and interviews for possible schools.

CONDITIONAL OBSTACLE: Business travel may conflict with course schedule.

HOW TO OVERCOME: Discuss with teacher and get assignments ahead of travel; arrange make-up classes; postpone unnecessary travel.

PSYCHOLOGICAL OBSTACLE: ''Learning a foreign language is difficult. I never studied language in high school or college.''

HOW TO OVERCOME: Sit in on a class to determine how difficult it will be to study; recognize that people do learn languages. Commit yourself to studying and doing what is necessary to learn the language.

5. *What's in it for me?:* ''After achieving this goal, I will be bilingual. I will be able to travel in France with more confidence. I will have a skill that makes me more promotable.''

TASK 4: FORMULATE ACTION PLANS

The final task of the goal-setting process incorporates Tasks 1 and 3 into a workable action plan. This plan details the activities and actions necessary to accomplish the goal. *Action plans* organize thoughts into logical and executable action items (objectives). They describe the objectives to be reached and the tactics to be used to achieve the desired expectations for each goal. When objectives and tactics are incorporated into a workable action plan, goal achievement is more likely to occur.

The formulation of a goal-oriented action plan starts with identifying opportunities for goal achievement (Task 1), creating S.M.A.R.T. goal statements that are correctly constructed and documented (Task 2), and fully developing goals (Task 3).

The first step in the creation of a written action plan is a final review of the goal information available to ensure that it is complete, clear and realistic enough to serve as the foundation for focused action and activity. When you have gathered the basic material for each goal and goal statement, ask the following questions:

- Is the goal complementary to the mission? Does it contribute to the overall purpose?

- Is the goal realistic? Is it practical, achievable and possible?

- Did the individuals responsible for achieving the goal participate in its creation? (Commitment is a component of success.)

- Have outcomes been quantified so that progress can be measured? This should include when and how much progress is expected.

- Are the objectives defined for reaching the goal? How will the goal be achieved?

- Are sufficient resources committed for reaching the goal? Resources should include the required people, funding, equipment, commitment, etc.

- Are potential obstacles to the goal identified? Have contingency plans been designed?

If you can answer "yes" to each of these questions, then the action plan will provide a road map to goal achievement.

Each of the above elements will be scattered throughout the working papers and goal statements developed in the earlier tasks of the goal-setting process.

The purpose of formulating an action plan is to provide order and organization to the important details of each goal. Order and organization are best achieved using the action-planning form shown on the next page. This form helps to create a road map to goal accomplishment.

GOAL ACTION FORM

Once a review is finished and there is reasonable assurance that all (or most) of the necessary goal-oriented details exist, then the Goal Action Form can be completed. It is useful because it documents the action plan for goal achievement.

Goal Action Form

GOAL:	RATIONALE FOR THIS GOAL:

ACTION PLAN: (Steps/Procedures/Assignments)   **DEADLINES:**

1.   1.

2.   2.

3.   3.

4.   4.

PROJECTED RESULTS (Success Indicators):

☐ Immediate:

☐ Long Term:

OBSTACLES/CONSTRAINTS:

COST (Dollars, Personnel Time):

PERSON RESPONSIBLE:	COMPLETION DATE:

COMPLETING THE GOAL ACTION FORM

There are eight separate entry areas of the Goal Action Form. Each information element was outlined, defined or acquired during the earlier tasks of opportunity identification, goal statement creation and goal development. The information required is

☐ Goal

Enter the actual goal statement created in Task 2. This statement contains S.M.A.R.T. goal elements: specific, measurable, action-oriented, realistic, and time- and resource-constrained.

☐ Rationale for This Goal

This is the goal benefit outlined in Task 1, Opportunity Identification; it describes the importance of the goal to the mission as a guide to the rationale.

If the goal type is

- *Essential:* The goal is necessary for continued growth and progress of the business or individual.

- *Problem-solving:* Proposes a more appropriate or desired condition than the condition that exists. It eliminates a problem that hinders growth, progress, creativity, improvement, etc.

- *Innovative:* Makes something already good or satisfactory quantifiably better, faster, cheaper, easier, safer, etc.

The goal rationale should also include the W.I.I.F.M. (What's In It For Me?) identified in goal development. The personal benefit to goal achievement (especially in a business environment) is an important motivator that ensures success.

☐ Action Plan (Steps/Procedures/Assignments)

This lists the specific objectives that must be met. This is the most important aspect of the action plan because it outlines the specific and measurable steps to take to reach the goal, as well as the methods to be used. This section should also include the approaches (tactics) necessary to satisfy the needs for goal achievement.

Deadlines — Deadlines provide a time limitation allowed for completion of objectives and the goal. Precise deadlines encourage activity and establish the priority of each objective.

COMPLETING THE GOAL ACTION FORM
(continued)

☐ Projected Results (Success Indicators)

These are the long- and short-term expected results that indicate progress and/or completion of the objectives and the goal. These quantifiable elements provide a standard for comparison and milestones for measuring progress.

☐ Obstacles/Constraints

These are the potential physical, conditional and psychological obstacles that could block progress to the goal. Include the contingency plan and tactics necessary to overcome these obstacles.

☐ Cost (Dollars, Personnel Time)

State the allowable expense for achieving the goal in dollars and resources to be used. A cost and resource constraint ensures that an acceptable return on investment exists for this goal.

☐ Person Responsible

This identifies who is responsible for achieving the goal. Many individuals participate in achieving specific objectives, but only one individual can be held accountable for goal accomplishment.

☐ Completion Date

State the exact date and time for goal completion. This information is part of a properly constructed goal statement.

The completed Goal Action Form organizes the various elements of the goal into an orderly, workable road map for goal achievement. It provides a visual representation (and reminder) of all the actions, activities, expected results, timing, benefits, responsibilities and contingencies of a well-planned goal.

TASK 4: SUMMARY

Action plans bring all the elements of goals together to create a useful road map to goal achievement.

Achievement of goals has a better chance for success when the goals are

✔ Clear, realistic, and complementary to the mission

✔ Correctly constructed and documented

✔ Properly developed

✔ Supported by workable objectives

✔ Incorporated into a written action plan

Goal Action Forms are helpful devices for organizing the diverse elements of goals into a complete and integrated package.

The form provided on page 66 provides a handy reference and reminder sheet for ensuring goal accomplishment.

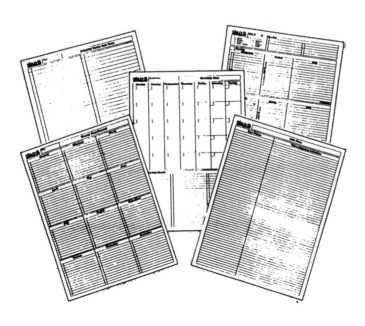

Goal Setting in Practice: Task 4

Remember: The action plan is your road map to goal achievement. Plan each step. Clearly define and state the actions and activities necessary for reaching your goal. A plan helps you take action in a way that ensures goal achievement.

P A R T

IV

Goal Achievement

THE FOUNDATION AND SUPPORT FOR GOAL ACHIEVEMENT

The four tasks—(1) identify opportunities, (2) write goal statements, (3) develop goals, and (4) formulate action plans—are only the foundation and support activities for goal achievement. They lay the groundwork for goal achievement by setting the stage for success.

Goals are achieved only through actions and activities. Plans and planning are very important parts of the goal-achievement process. Good planning can tell you how and where to go—but it won't help you succeed unless you put the plan into action.

There are three action elements necessary to ensure goal achievement:

1. **Implement** the plan—the programs, procedures, policies, etc.

2. **Monitor** progress made at specific intervals.

3. **Revise** objectives as necessary.

When executed properly, these three elements create a self-correcting loop for goal accomplishment.

IMPLEMENT THE PLAN

Planning is a good start on the road to goal accomplishment. The new ideas, procedures, policies and programs, however, must be implemented for progress to be made. Without action, nothing is achieved.

It is easier to take action when you have completed the Goal Action Form, because it serves as the road map that specifies who, what, when, how and how much for each goal.

WHO is assigned the responsibility for coordinating the activities needed for reaching OBJECTIVES

WHAT is to be accomplished

WHEN the activity must be completed

HOW the goal will be achieved and what obstacles/constraints could block achievement of the goal

HOW MUCH the cost is in dollars, resources, and personnel time to be expended to achieve the goal

All the elements of the Goal Action Form outline the actions necessary for goal accomplishment. However, only real actions and activities will accomplish the goal.

The Chinese have a proverb,

> *The journey of 10,000 miles starts with but a single step.*

Goals cannot be achieved solely through planning and wishing. Goal accomplishment requires action and implementation of the positive programs, procedures and policies that make it possible to achieve the desired goal.

MONITOR PROGRESS

Achieving the established objectives and goals requires careful periodic monitoring of the actions taken and the measurable results of the actions.

Monitoring confirms that time and effort are productive in achieving the intended results. Also, when you monitor actions and progress, you will see which tactics work best.

The quantifiable and measurable standards of performance established in the goal statement and the milestones (dates) set for review help provide tangible ways to monitor progress.

It is important to set the monitoring milestones at practical and planned intervals. They should be clear and precise calendar dates for review that can be understood by those who are responsible for accomplishing objectives.

The Goal Action Form serves as an excellent checklist for monitoring progress toward objective and goal achievement. Each of these planned elements can be used periodically to review the actual progress made (plan vs. actual).

The monitoring function is a very important element in goal accomplishment because it will indicate whether midcourse adjustments to objectives and tactics are needed to ensure success.

REVISE OBJECTIVES

To achieve your goals, you sometimes have to revise your objectives and tactics, because the actions and activities taken do not always produce results exactly as planned. Sometimes results fall short of planned expectations.

Part of goal development (Task 3) was to identify obstacles to goal achievement and methods for overcoming each potential obstacle. Even with proper planning and established contingency plans, new, unidentified obstacles occur that require changes in direction or method to reach the goal. It may be vitally important to the ultimate achievement of the goal to revise your objectives and tactics.

It's very important to note that the goals themselves should not be changed. The goal is important, or it would not be this far along in the process. The monitoring activity outlined above will identify the most effective tactics—those that produce the most beneficial results.

Circumstances change and so should the plans, objectives and tactics you use to achieve worthwhile goals. Continually review and revise your Goal Action Form (ideally, once every three months for long-term goals). This creates a useful and dynamic work plan for accomplishing your goals.

Goal achievement occurs only when the following two major and seven minor elements are present:

I. Comprehensive Goal Foundation

1. Identified goal opportunities
2. S.M.A.R.T. goal statements
3. Complete goal development
4. Written action plan

II. Goal Achievement Activities

5. Implement program
6. Monitor results
7. Revise plan

REVISE OBJECTIVES (continued)

The cycle of implementing, monitoring and revising should be executed over and over during the goal achievement process. When you revise your objectives and tactics, you then have to implement a new set of policies, procedures and programs. This implementation is followed by additional monitoring activities at scheduled intervals that result in additional revisions, followed by new implementations, monitoring . . . and so on until each goal is achieved.

This cycle must occur as often as necessary to draw closer to achieving your goals. The cycle ends only when the goal is reached.

GOAL ACHIEVEMENT

Goals are achieved only through action and activity. The three actionable elements that ensure goal achievement are

✔ *Implement* — The who, what, when, how and how much definitions of action and activities are necessary for goal achievement. This represents the physical execution of the activities.

✔ *Monitor* — Review of progress toward goal achievement. Comparing your plan with actual progress. The use of quantifiable expected results and specific milestone dates for review.

✔ *Revise* — Revision of the objectives and tactics when change is indicated. Use tactics that work and draw you closer to your goal. *Do not revise the goal;* change only the means to achieving the goal—the objectives and tactics. Determine what works and what doesn't. Revise the action plan to be more productive.

SUMMARY: GOALS AND GOAL SETTING

What is a goal?

A goal is a specific and measurable accomplishment to be achieved within time and cost constraints.

Goals are written statements of intent and results to be achieved. These statements contain:

- Action verbs
- Measurable outcomes
- Specific dates for accomplishment
- Cost and resource constraints

Mission statements define your cause and provide direction for goals.

Objectives are tactics used to achieve goals. They must be complementary to the goal and the mission.

Why set goals?

Well-defined goals enable people to choose, design and implement their life and work objectives to achieve a mission or life purpose.

Goals will:

- Establish direction
- Identify results
- Improve teamwork
- Heighten performance

Who sets goals?

The parties involved in achieving the goal should help set the goal to ensure success. People are committed to achieving goals that they help create.

How are goals set?

Creating goals is a four-task process:

1. Identify opportunities for goals that evolve from what
   —"MUST BE DONE"—Essential GOALS
   —"OUGHT TO BE DONE"—Problem-Solving GOALS
   —"WE WOULD LIKE TO HAVE DONE"—Innovative GOALS

2. Write S.M.A.R.T. goal statements
   —Specific: Detailed, particular, focused
   —Measurable: Quantifiable, limiting
   —Action-oriented: Produce results
   —Realistic: Practical, achievable
   —Time- and resource-constrained: Scheduled, regulated by time and deadlines

3. Develop goals
   —Classify goals by type
   —Prioritize within each type
   —Establish standards for performance
   —Identify obstacles to goal achievement
   —Determine "W.I.I.F.M." (What's in it for me?)

4. Formulate action plans
   —Use the Goal Action Form as a road map to goal achievement.

How are goals achieved?

Goal achievement requires you to:

1. Implement the plan
   —Planning must be careful and comprehensive
   —Execute the plan

2. Monitor progress
   —Measure planned vs. actual results
   —Determine which elements work and do not work

3. Revise objectives
   —Change tactics, not goals
   —Apply what works

4. Restart the cycle
   —Implement the plan
   —Monitor progress
   —Revise objectives

Continue until your goal is achieved.   *SUCCESS!*

ANSWERS TO EXERCISES

Exercise #1

1. *Action verb:* gain.
   Measurable outcome: five new customers, gross sales of $20,000.
   Specific date: July 1, 1993.
   Cost constraint: within budget of $1,000.

2. *Action verb:* expand.
   Measurable outcome: market share of 5%.
   Specific date: December 31, 1993.
   Cost constraint: without increase in ad expense.

3. *Action verb:* secure.
   Measurable outcome: two new clients, $30,000 income.
   Specific date: June 30, 1993.
   Cost constraint: no more than 30% of time to service.

Exercise #3

- Statements A, D, and G are too general. They state only broad "intents for action."

- Statements B, E, and H are a little more specific, but not specific enough to be used in goal statements.

- Statements C, F, and I are more specific and focus intent on a desired outcome.

Exercise #4

Measurable outcomes:

A. The term "better" cannot be quantified as written. "Better" is a relative term and no indication is given as to what "better service" will mean for each specific customer.

B. "Five work days" is a measurable outcome. It can be determined whether an answer was or was not given in 4 days or 6 days after it was received.

C. "Significantly" is too ambiguous a term for goals. It is relative to an undefined standard.

D. "Fifty percent of current levels" is measurable, assuming the number of complaints received is known.

E. "Only very" is not measurable or quantifiable.

Exercise #5

Realistic statements:

A. Swimming a mile has been accomplished by many individuals. With practice, many people could achieve this goal.

D. Learning to play the piano is also an activity that has been demonstrated and is achievable.

Unrealistic statements:

B. Swimming across the Pacific Ocean is unrealistic, even for expert swimmers.

C. Although holding your breath until you faint is possible and achievable, the author's opinion is that it is impractical and therefore unrealistic. If there were a *legitimate purpose* for holding your breath until you faint, then perhaps this activity could be classified as realistic.

Exercise #6

The short-distance runner will gradually build endurance by running a little bit farther each day (the stretch). Eventually, endurance will build so that marathon distances are achievable.

Exercise #7

- Statements B, F, and G are specific enough to represent deadlines.

- Statements A and C are too general to be deadlines.

- Statements D and E at first appear to be deadlines, but unfortunately the words ''first thing'' and ''before the close'' can be interpreted differently by different people.

Deadlines for goals must leave no room for interpretation.

Author's Comments

Top-down goal setting increases the risk that those at lower levels who are directly responsible for achieving the goal will be left out of the necessary discussion, compromise and agreement cycle that helps to ensure success.

The individuals responsible for goal accomplishment must participate in the goal setting process in order to buy into the commitments to goal achievement that are established at higher levels.

If goals are dictated, individuals at lower levels may feel less responsible for goal achievement. They are more committed to achieving goals that they help define and establish.

Bottom-up goal setting may not establish the levels necessary to maintain a viable business enterprise. For example, the individuals may not commit to the performance levels necessary to provide enough sales, profit or cash flow to keep the company in business.

Which Is Best: Top-Down or Bottom-Up?

The method used to establish goals—top-down or bottom-up—is less important than the process used to determine the goals to be achieved. The goal-setting process must include discussion, compromise and agreement that all levels can endorse and support to accomplish the goals.

Top-down goal setting can be effective if management enlists the help and support of people in the lower levels of the organization to determine what the targets (goals) should be. This should not be a dictatorial process, but rather a cooperative effort to choose the proper level of need, commitment and action necessary to achieve the goals that are ultimately established.

For bottom-up goal setting, the people at lower levels must understand the needs of the organization as a whole. This understanding must be of sufficient depth to enable them to establish and commit to goals that result in progress for the organization. Upper levels of the organization can best provide this knowledge through open and continual communication.

Regardless of how the goals are set (top-down or bottom-up), the key ingredient is the dialogue and understanding that occurs between the levels involved.

Physical Obstacles

Some possible alternatives for overcoming the physical obstacle of a word processing system that becomes inoperative are

- Arranging ahead of time with a word processing service to help absorb the extra work should your system become unusable.

- Having manual typewriters and extra temporary typists available for use should the automated system not function.

Changing Objectives

The thoughts for changing objectives must be concerned with "how" to reach the goal. The goal of "40 letters per day by June 30, 1993" cannot be changed. Therefore, you must change the "how."

Once again, think of manual typewriters, more temporary employees assigned or using overtime hours until the problems are fixed.

Conditional Obstacles

Conditional obstacles like this one might be overcome by changing the work hours and/or the workday schedule. You might also temporarily relax the standards of performance until the crisis passes.

Remember that efforts may have to be redoubled after conditions return to normal in order to get back on track and maintain progress to the goal.

Psychological Obstacles

Methods for overcoming psychological obstacles include

- Conducting a meeting that stresses the possibilities for reaching the goal. Get everyone to express their viewpoints, especially any doubters. As a group, develop a positive attitude to goal achievement.

- Recalling a past goal that was achieved that also *appeared* to be unreachable.

- Remembering that goals established by those responsible for achieving them have a much better chance for success. Psychological obstacles can sometimes be avoided by a bottom-up goal-setting process.

We hope you enjoyed this book. If so, we have good news for you. This title is part of the best-selling *FIFTY-MINUTE*™ *Series* of books. All *Series* books are similar in size and identical in price. Several are supported with training videos (identified by the symbol ❶ next to the title).

FIFTY-MINUTE Books and Videos are available from your distributor. A free catalog is available upon request from Crisp Publications, Inc., 1200 Hamilton Court, Menlo Park, California 94025.

FIFTY-MINUTE Series Books & Videos organized by general subject area.

Management Training:

Small Business & Financial Planning:

Adult Literacy & Learning:

Career/Retirement & Life Planning: